ABC'S OF EMOTIONS

DEDICATED

to Sami, Max, Ryan, and my mom.

Written by Amanda Minuk
Assembled and designed by Amanda Minuk

All graphics and images from Canva.com
Canva contributors: Amazed (Icons54), Angry (BNPDesignStudio), Annoyed (Marmalade Moon), Anxious (djvstock), Bored (BNPDesignStudio), Brave (curvabezier), Calm (Andres Rodriguez), Confident (barsrsind), Confused (Marmalade Moon), Determined (Roundicons Pro), Disappointed (Icons8), Disgusted (Icons8), Elated (Phuriphat Chanchonabot), Embarrased (Alena Nikolaeva), Excited (Icons54), Friendly (Roundicons Pro), Frightened (iconixar), Frustrated (Roundicons Pro), Glad (Chanut is industries), Grateful (Twemoji) , Great (BNPDesignStudio), Grumpy (Yayayoyo); Hangry (Dimensions Design), Happy (sparkle stroke), irate (studiog), Jealous (Royyan Wijaya), Joking (Twemoji), Kind (Liara Studio), Lazy (jemastock2), Lonely (vecstock), Loving (Marmalade Moon), Mad (cherry icon), Nervous (vecstock), Nice (Yayayoyo), Optimistic (Yayayoyo), Overwhelmed (Yayayoyo) Pity (Marmalade Moon), Quiet (liliasu), Relaxed (liliasu), Relieved (Yayayoyo) , Sad (vecstock), Satisfied (vecstock), Scared (Andres Rodriguez), Shy (icon54), Silly (iconsolid), Sleepy (vecstock), Surprised (vecstock), Tired (Icon54), Tricky (vecstock), Uncomfortable (Yayayoyo) , Unsure (Yayayoyo), Valued (Yayayoyo), Wild (creativepriyanka), Worried (vectortradition), Xenodochial (Roundicons Pro), Yucky (gstudioimagen2), Yummy (Iconsolid), Zany (Icons8)

ISBN 978-1-7777779-1-3

ABC'S OF EMOTIONS

By: Amanda Minuk

How are you
feeling today?
I hope it's :)

A. M___

Aa

is for

Amaz**ed**   An**gry**   Ann**oyed**   Anxi**ous**

Bb
is for

Bored   Brave

Cc

is for

Calm   Confident   Confused

Dd

is for

Deter**mi**ned   **Dis**a**ppo**inted   **Disg**us**t**ed

Ee

is for

Elated   Embarrassed   Excited

Ff

is for

Friendly   **Frightened**   **Frustrated**

Gg

is for

Glad   Grateful   Great   Grumpy

Hh

is for

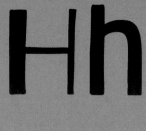

Han**gry**   Ha**ppy**

Ii

is for

Irate

Jj
is for

Jealous

Joking

Kk

is for

kind

Ll

is for

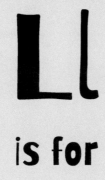

Lazy   Lonely   Loving

Mm

is for

Mad

Nn

is for

Nervous

Nice

Oo

is for

Optimistic

Overwhelmed

Pp
is for

Pity

Qq

is for

Quiet

Rr

is for

Relaxed   **Re**lieved

Ss

is for

Sad   Satisfied   Scared   Shy

Ss

is for

Silly   Sleepy   Surprised

Tt
is for

Tired   Tricky

Uu
is for

Uncomfortable

Unsure

Vv

is for

Valued

Ww

is for

Wild

Worried

Xx

is for

Xenodochial
(Friendly to strangers)

Yy

is for

Yucky   Yummy

Zz

is for

Zany

Manufactured by Amazon.ca
Bolton, ON

23782712R00019